PRAYER
FOR A CHILD

BY RACHEL FIELD

PICTURES BY ELIZABETH ORTON JONES

Simon & Schuster Books for Young Readers

SIMON & SCHUSTER BOOKS FOR YOUNG READERS
An imprint of Simon & Schuster Children's Publishing Division
Simon & Schuster Macmillan
1230 Avenue of the Americas
New York, New York 10020
Library of Congress catalog card number:
44–47191

ISBN 0-02-735190-4

Printed in the United States of America

35 34 33 32 31 30 29 28 27

FOR HANNAH

PRAYER FOR A CHILD

Bless this milk and bless this bread.
Bless this soft and waiting bed
Where I presently shall be
Wrapped in sweet security.
Through the darkness, through the night
Let no danger come to fright
My sleep till morning once again
Beckons at the window pane.
Bless the toys whose shapes I know,
The shoes that take me to and fro
Up and down and everywhere.
Bless my little painted chair.
Bless the lamplight, bless the fire,
Bless the hands that never tire
In their loving care of me.
Bless my friends and family.
Bless my Father and my Mother
And keep us close to one another.
Bless other children, far and near,
And keep them safe and free from fear.
So let me sleep and let me wake
In peace and health, for Jesus' sake.
                                            Amen.

**B**less this milk and bless this bread.

**less** this soft and waiting bed
Where I presently shall be
Wrapped in sweet security

Through the darkness, through the night
Let no danger come to fright
My sleep till morning once again
Beckons at the window pane

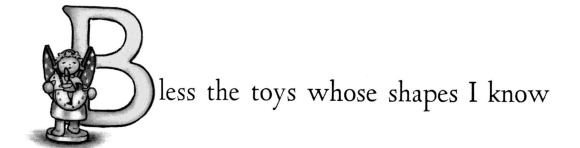

less the toys whose shapes I know

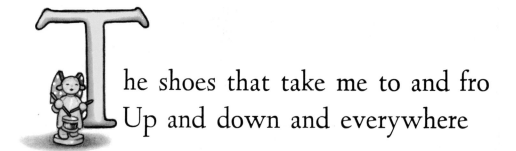

The shoes that take me to and fro
Up and down and everywhere

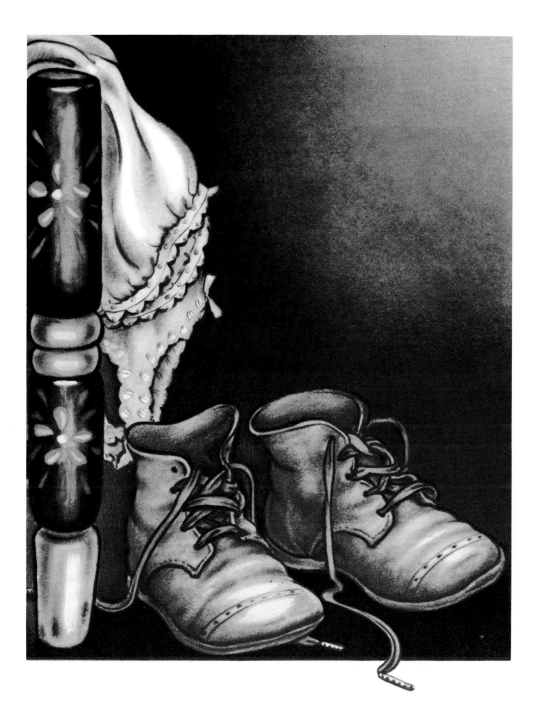

less my little painted chair

less the lamplight, bless the fire

less the hands that never tire
In their loving care of me

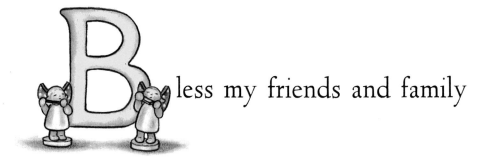 less my friends and family

less my Father and my Mother
And keep us close to one another

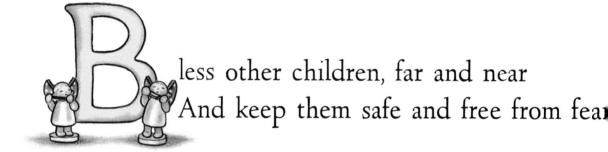

Bless other children, far and near
And keep them safe and free from fear

So let me sleep and let me wake
In peace and health, for Jesus' sake

men